Brad Power

ISIS & Al QAIDA

in Egypt of Al Sisi

Zionist *Jerusalem Post* wrote:

"Abdel Fattah al-Sisi is the Egyptian people's special gift to the State of Israel. We are talking about a worthy leader who projects strength, confidence, and authority."

An Extraordinary Analysis of *Best Seller Books'* Writer
Brad Power

INDEX

Egypt's Terror Threat

Egypt faces a serious threat from terrorist groups, not only in the Sinai Peninsula but also in other parts of the country. Unfortunately, the government's counter-terrorism campaign over the past several years has not ended this threat, and some of its policies have actually contributed to the problem. In order for Egypt to succeed in defeating terrorism, it needs to develop a more comprehensive approach that involves more nimble and selective security tactics, economic policies that provide disaffected Bedouin youth in Sinai with meaningful alternatives to joining the terrorists' ranks, and more open political space in the country to allow for the airing of grievances without fear of retribution.

Statistics show that incidents of terrorist violence have spiked from an average of 30 per month in 2014 to an average of 100 per month from January to August 2015. In addition, the major terrorist group in North Sinai, Ansar Bayt al-Maqdis—now calling itself Wilayat Sinai, the "Sinai Province" of the Islamic State—has grown more sophisticated in its attacks and has taken on aspects of an insurgency. On July 1 of this year, it staged a series of coordinated attacks in the North Sinai region, even taking over the town of Sheikh Zuweid for several hours. Wilayat Sinai's forces killed a large, disputed number of soldiers and police before the terrorists were forced to retreat.

In mainland Egypt, groups like Ajnad Misr and the Allied Popular Resistance Movement, some of whose members are believed to be former Muslim Brotherhood youth activists who grew disillusioned with the Brotherhood's longstanding position on nonviolence, have attacked regime officials, economic infrastructure, and police. Reports of attacks have increased in the Cairo area and in the governorates of Fayoum and Sharqia.

The government has responded so far with brute force against the terrorists, but reports of terrorist "kills" by security forces belie the actual situation on the ground. For example, on September 23, the government announced that it was winding down a 16-day operation in the North Sinai region that purportedly killed scores of terrorists. The government claimed this campaign had "achieved its goals" in destroying terrorist hideouts. Yet brute force, including punishment of whole villages if one or two youths were believed to have joined militant groups, has had the effect of alienating large segments of the North Sinai population. Not only have such policies probably contributed more recruits to Wilayat Sinai, but they have also hindered the government's ability to collect intelligence on the terrorists.

If the mostly Bedouin residents of Sinai see the government as their enemy, what incentive is there for them to inform on their fellow residents who are aiding the terrorists? Granted, the brutality of Wilayat Sinai has had a chilling effect on such possible cooperation—there have been reports of the terrorists killing alleged government informants and dumping beheaded bodies along a roadside as a warning to others—but extensive studies by counter-terrorism experts have shown that unless a government can win the support of the local population, it will be unable to successfully put down a terrorist insurgency.

The Egyptian government needs to recalibrate how it approaches the terrorism problem not only in Sinai but elsewhere in Egypt. This involves a more targeted security response—going after actual terrorists as opposed to villagers suspected of being sympathetic to Wilayat Sinai—and creating economic opportunities for Bedouin youth so that they will not be attracted to the entreaties of terrorists.

The Bedouin of the Sinai Peninsula have long been a neglected group. Part of the problem stems from the fact that many Nile Valley Egyptians see them as not full citizens and not to be fully trusted, stemming from stereotypes that they are smugglers as well as collaborators with Israel during that country's occupation of the region. Partly as a result, the Bedouin are prohibited from joining the military and the police forces. Hence, outside of subsistence agriculture, they have few avenues to make a living. Tourist jobs in the South Sinai, for example, are frequently reserved for mainland Egyptians.

The government needs to allow Bedouin youth, after proper vetting, to join the police forces in Sinai. Not only will this provide sorely needed jobs to the youth, but it will also provide the government with valuable intelligence on the terrorists because such residents would know the terrain and the populace. The government should also establish training programs for Bedouin youth to enter the tourism industry in South Sinai. In addition, it should provide tax incentives for labor-intensive industries in North Sinai. The government would have to protect the businesses and their workers from possible terrorist attacks, but the costs would be worth it if they succeed in drawing disaffected youth away from the terrorists.

Outside Sinai, the government also needs to end some of its repressive policies that have alienated significant segments of the population. For example, checks on assembly in the draconian protest law and restrictions on the press—including stiff fines on journalists who do not parrot the government's reporting on terrorist incidents—in the new counter-terrorism law should be rescinded. Security personnel who commit abuses—whether against protesters in the streets of Cairo or against villagers in Sinai—should be held accountable. With a new parliament to be seated soon, the government should also allow opposition politicians to freely criticize government policies without being labeled as traitors. A more open political environment will work to dispel the notion that violence is the only avenue for political change.

On the ideological front, President Abdel-Fattah El Sisi is to be commended for calling on Islamic religious figures to do a better job confronting the messages of the terrorists, but the government needs to think more creatively in this realm. Using rehabilitated terrorists to speak informally to young people in danger of radicalization may be a more effective way of reaching this segment of the population than via state-run religious bodies.

Egypt's friends in the international community also should play a role in helping it develop a more comprehensive counter-terrorism program. The United States should continue to aid Egypt militarily and offer equipment and training that is geared to counter-terrorism operations. If the Egyptian government is reluctant to follow U.S. advice on counter-terrorism best practices, then Egypt's regional friends and benefactors, like Saudi Arabia and the United Arab Emirates, should be encouraged to weigh in with Cairo.

The United States and the European Union should help the government to develop North Sinai economically. Although U.S. economic assistance to Egypt is lower now than it was in the 1990s, the U.S. administration should be able to make a compelling case to Congress, on national security grounds, that a special economic fund should be created to help create job opportunities in this area to weaken an Islamic State affiliate.

Egypt is a pivotal country in a volatile region. Helping Egypt succeed in its counter-terrorism efforts will not only help the Egyptian people but will deal a significant blow to region-wide extremist movements. But in order for this to come about, the Egyptian government will have to adopt a holistic approach to combating terrorism.

Abdel-Fattah Al Sisi

Sisi is a product of the military system: He attended the Air Force's high school as a cadet, graduated from Egypt's Military Academy (al-Kuliya al-Harbiya), and rose steadily through the ranks. He held a succession of senior positions within the military, both administrative and unit commands, becoming Commander of the Northern Military Zone in February 2008. Sisi was appointed as the Director of Military Intelligence in January 2010 after serving a stint as deputy director of the same agency. In that capacity, Sisi openly spoke about the use of virginity tests on female protesters in Tahrir Square in March 2011, and promised in June that they would not be used again.

Following the deaths of 16 Egyptian soldiers in Sinai in August 2012, Egypt's newly-elected President Muhammad Morsi forced the resignation of several senior military officials, including Defense Minister Field Marshal Hussein al-Tantawy and Chief of Staff General Sami Hafez Anan. Sisi was promoted to full general and appointed as minister of defense and commander-in-chief of the armed forces. Sisi was actively engaged in the fight against terrorism in the Sinai, visiting the region to inspect security facilities.

Despite early rumors that he had been appointed because of his sympathy for Morsi's Muslim Brotherhood—Sisi's personal piety is well-known—Sisi warned as early as January, as the military intervened to quell unrest in the Suez Canal, that political events could lead to the "collapse of the state." In April 2013, apparently speaking off-the-cuff, Sisi said, "Any hand stretched against Egypt must be cut off." Both supporters and opponents of the Brotherhood interpreted his words as supporting their positions.

Notable responses to security crises during Sisi's period as Defense Minister include the strikes against militants in August 2012 and the more measured response following the abduction of troops in May 2013.

As the possibility of mass protests on June 30, 2013 became evident, Sisi said that, while the army would remain neutral in any dispute, it would not allow the country to descend into chaos; after the first day and a half of protests, the military released a statement giving political factions 48 hours to negotiate a power-sharing deal. On July 3, the military forced Morsi from office and installed Judge Adly Mansour as interim president.

Less than a month later, Sisi called for mass demonstrations supporting a mandate for the military to fight terrorism. The military-led government used these marches as justification of their crackdown on pro-Brotherhood protesters in Cairo and other cities, which reached the peak of violence during the bloody clearing of the Raba'a al-Adaweya and Nahda protest camps, as well as continuing their violent opposition to militants in Sinai. The efficacy of the government's attempts to eradicate violent opposition are debatable: Attacks on government forces throughout Egypt have been the norm since Sisi became the de facto leader of the government in July 2013, and have continued through his formal inauguration in June 2014.

Soldiers of Egypt (Ajnad Misr)

Ajnad Misr is the only terrorist group operating exclusively in the Greater Cairo area. The group typically relies on the use of primitive weaponry, including homemade IEDs, to execute its attacks.

On January 23, 2014, Ajnad Misr declared its presence with a tweet: "In the name of God the Merciful, may He stand beside us." The following day, the group released their first statement where they claimed responsibility for several attacks as early as November 20, 2013, and began a media campaign, "Retribution is Life," which they promoted as a twitter hashtag (in Arabic).

Since this time, Ajnad Misr has been the most active terrorist group operating in Egypt outside of the Sinai Peninsula.On May 12, 2014, the Ministry of Interior announced that it had apprehended and obtained confessions from Ajnad operatives in Giza. The Ministry released video confessions of the alleged terrorists. These confessions, however, have not been independently verified, and often similar confessions are elicited under threat of torture.

Ajnad Misr differs from other terrorist groups operating in Egypt in that it does not fully insist on the establishment of an Islamic caliphate. Ajnad Misr recognizes the legitimacy of Egypt as a distinct nation (as opposed to the Islamic umma). The group also employs the language of the January 25, 2011 revolution, lamenting that "the goals of the revolution" have not been fulfilled. Despite this difference, the group has adopted language in its statements that would align it with a Salafi jihadi ideology, and the group quotes Ibn Taymiyyah, an Islamic scholar from the Middle Ages whose teachings have greatly influenced Salafism.

Also unlike some other jihadi groups (particularly those affiliated with Al Qaeda), Ajnad Misr takes a sympathetic view toward civilians, even those in opposition to the group. Ajnad Misr directs its hostilities toward state actors; although several of the terror acts for which it has claimed responsibility have also resulted in the loss of civilian lives, the group claims to avoid this at all costs. (Ansar Bayt al-Maqdis, for instance, does claim to avoid civilians, however they do not hesitate to claim attacks in which there are high civilian death tolls.)

The group specifically targets particular individuals whom it sees as offenders; this included Brigadier General Ahmed Zaki, killed in an April 23, 2014 attack, and whom the group condemned for his complicity in the arrest and torture of Egyptian youth.

The group takes particular issue with the Egyptian state's treatment of women, referencing abuse of female protesters and promising retribution to the mothers of those who had been killed at the hands of the state.

In this sense, Ajnad Misr's ideological and operational logic falls somewhere between a traditional insurgency and the Salafi jihadi groups operating in the Sinai. Regardless of any possible ideological differences, Ansar Bayt al-Maqdis has declared Ajnad Misr to be their "brothers."

According to TIMEP's data, Ajnad Misr has claimed at least 15 attacks in Greater Cairo, many of which have been targeted toward particular police officers and/or their vehicles.

Ajnad Misr's first coordinated attack took place on January 24, 2014, when a series of bombs exploded on the eve of the anniversary of the start 2011 uprising that resulted in the ouster of Hosni Mubarak. Ajnad Misr claimed responsibility for two attacks on police in Giza, killing eight and wounding over 90. Ansar Bayt al-Maqdis also claimed responsibility for the attacks, although they later ceded at least partial credit to Ajnad Misr.

On April 2, 2014, Ajnad Misr executed a series of bombings at Cairo University, killing a police officer and wounding others.

On the year anniversary of massive protests calling for Morsi's ouster, Ajnad Misr planned a series of explosions occurred outside Ittihadeya Palace in Heliopolis. A Ministry of Interior explosives expert was killed while trying to defuse an explosive that detonated and other personnel were injured. A second bomb exploded an hour later, injuring a policeman. The third explosion killed another explosives expert who was trying to defuse an explosive device. Ajnad Misr had announced these attacks via social media and later claimed to have defused some of the devices in order to minimize civilian casualties.

Popular Resistance Movement

The group operates throughout the country, with attacks by affiliates from Luxor to North Sinai. Affiliates are most active in greater Cairo and the Nile Delta region, including Alexandria, as well as Fayoum and Beni Suef.

The Popular Resistance Movement is an affiliation of local actors and groups across Egypt that have typically utilized low levels of violence in order to combat both the Egyptian security apparatus and those they have seen as supportive of what they describe as "the coup," referencing the military-backed ouster of former President Muhammad Morsi.

The majority of attacks that the group has claimed are focused on government institutions (including the police and military) and economic targets. The group typically carries out low-violence attacks using rudimentary weapons, including crude improvised explosives, Molotov cocktails, and stun or "sound" grenades. While the group utilizes social media platforms such as Facebook and Twitter, this utilization is often unsophisticated and uncoordinated when compared to better-organized groups like Ajnad Misr or Wilayat Sinai.

The Popular Resistance Movement does not operate under clear leadership. The larger movement is divided across multiple cities, regions, and actors with no identifiable central core.

The group's first public statement was spread through media associated with the Muslim Brotherhood, prompting speculation that the founders were disaffected Brotherhood youth, but the group's official pages did not make an explicit claim to that effect and the relationship cannot be confirmed.

There was an outburst of activity resembling that of the Popular Resistance Movement after the ouster of Muhammad Morsi in July 2013, but the movement emerged under its current name via a Facebook page created on January 25, 2014. On August 15, 2014, the group announced its intention to target security forces and the Popular Resistance Movement's Facebook page was shut down by site administrators the same. At that time, the group also claimed to have broadcast a message over a national radio network, but that has not been confirmed.

The group has targeted the police and military, setting police stations and security vehicles on fire. The group also carries out disruptive acts such as torching cars in abandoned lots or blocking off roads with burning tires. While initially the group's efforts showed an aversion to harming civilians, the nature of the attacks have escalated in terms of violence, including more sophisticated bombs being placed in cars near posted security guards or patrolling policemen and in areas with higher civilian presence.

Since the beginning of 2015, there has been a shift to the group's focus on economic targets, specifically international corporations such as communications companies Etisalat, Mobinil, and Vodafone and also international bank branches such as Emirates NBD banks. Additionally, there was also a rash of attacks on KFC restaurants in the region, including one attack that resulted in the death of an employee. There is evidence that many of these recent attacks were aimed at projecting a perception of economic and security instability in order to scare away foreign investors leading up to the economic conference in Sharm el-Sheikh in March 2015.

The disparate nature of the allied movement does not lend itself to a rigid official ideology; however, its discourse is best described as "religiously nationalist" rather than jihadist, as the ideology revolves around nationalist causes like retribution for Morsi's removal from power, rather than the jihadist mission of a unified caliphate or combating worldwide oppression of Muslims.

The group displays tendencies toward anti-capitalism and conservative Salafism, which also indicate a potential reason behind the shift of tactics away from pursuing government and particularly police targets toward the targeting of economic interests.

While there are indications of ties between the Popular Resistance Movement and the Muslim Brotherhood, the extent of these links is unclear. It is, however, clear that the movement opposes the current Egyptian government and those they view as supporters of "the coup" removing Morsi from power. This includes foreign—particularly Emirati—companies that the group sees as bringing foreign economic intervention to Egypt, as well as domestic businesses and business leaders (making direct reference to Naguib Sawiris).

On February 3, 2015, authorities disarmed two rudimentary bombs found at Cairo International Airport. The Popular Resistance Movement claimed responsibility for placing these bombs and stated that their placement was to coincide with the arrival of Ginny Rometty, Chairwoman of IBM, to Egypt, possibly as an attempt to scare foreign investors.

On February 10, the group claimed a series of attacks on police stations in Alexandria. News reports indicated that ten people were injured in five separate IED attacks.

Revolutionary Punishment claimed credit for two attacks in Luxor in mid-March. One was an attack on the local court complex that wounded two; the other was a claimed attack on a police checkpoint in the area that destroyed a police vehicle and reportedly killed its passengers. The second attack was not widely reported.

On Tuesday, April 21, the Execution Battalion—alternatively called the "Execution Movement" or "Execution Battalion Movement"—carried out a highly coordinated assassination on a police colonel and his conscript. After gunning down the victims in a Cairo suburb, the assailants exploded a diversionary device and fled.

Al Qaeda in the Sinai Peninsula

The group is very loyal to Al-Qaeda, and according to local terror experts, is in possession of advanced weapons, including man-portable air-defense systems (MANPADS) and mortars.

Ramzi Mahmoud al-Mowafi – Al-Mowafi, also known as "The Chemist" is well-known for being the personal physician of Osama Bin Laden. He spent a significant amount of time with Al-Qaeda in Afghanistan, where he worked as an explosives and chemical weapons expert. Al-Mowafi was serving a life sentence for unknown charges when he escaped in the infamous January 2011 Wadi al-Natroun prison break.

After breaking out of prison in January 2011, by August 2011, Egyptian intelligence officials declared that al-Mowafi had reappeared in the Sinai, offering trainings to militants from Jaysh al-Islam and Takfir wal-Hijra. On December 1, 2011, a statement on a jihadi web forum announced the formation of the group, "Ansar al-Jihad in the Sinai Peninsula."

Ansar al-Jihad considers itself the military wing of Al-Qaeda in the Sinai Peninsula, and indeed it appears to have the closest formal ties through al-Mowafi's connections. After announcing its foundation, the group declared its allegiance to Ayman al-Zawahiri, whom they called their "beloved Mujahid sheikh."

Al-Qaeda's ideology is reflected in the statements of Ansar al-Jihad, which call for war against foreign elements present in Muslim lands, particularly targeting the United States and Israel.

Ansar al-Jihad has claimed a series of gas pipeline attacks, including an attack on May 2, 2012, in retaliation for the death of one of its leaders in a Cairo prison.

While Ansar al-Jihad never formally claimed responsibility for the attack, a brutal August 19, 2013 attack on Central Security Forces has been linked to the group; 25 soldiers were executed while being transported between Al Arish and Rafah. Adel Mohamed Ibrahim, also known as Adel Habara, was arrested in

Arish on August 31, 2013. Habara, who has suspected ties to Ansar al-Jihad, confessed to having led the massacre.

Ansar Bayt al-Maqdis

The majority of the group's operations have taken place in North Sinai, but it has also claimed attacks in greater Cairo, Daqhalia, South Sinai, Matruh, Qalyubia, New Valley, and Ismailia.

Given the group's heightened operational security, its exact size, membership composition, and organizational structure are subject to speculation. Some intelligence assessments have estimated its size at around 1,000 members; first-hand accounts of the Sheikh Zuweid assault put its numbers at a few hundred. While official statements suggest that counterterrorism initiatives like "Operation Martyr's Right" have substantially reduced its numbers, the group's continued operational capacity underscores its ability to quickly replace lost fighters. It should be noted, however, that these fighters are both vetted (presumably for prolonged periods) and subject to ideological and paramilitary training, the lengths of which would likely impede this efficient replacement.

Regardless of exact numbers, the group is undeniably the most coordinated and operationally effective group in Egypt. Likely sometime in 2011, Tawfik Muhammad Freij Ziyada (a.k.a. Abu Abdullah) co-founded Ansar Bayt al-Maqdis with a number of jihadist elements; according to reports, many of these individuals, including followers of organizations like Tawhid wal-Jihad, met in prison sometime before the January 25 Revolution. Tawfik's deputy, Muhammad Ali Afifi Bedawi Nasif, and Muhammad al-Said Hassan Ibrahim al-Toukhi (more commonly known as Abu Obayda" transformed the nascent group into a conglomerate of regionally- and functionally-oriented cells.

Built around a number of second-tier leadership figures like Ahmed Muhammad Abdel Aziz al-Sigini, Mahmoud Muhammad Suleiman, and the recently killed Ashraf Ali Hasanain al-Gharably, regional cells operated at that time within their respective jurisdictional purviews. These satellites included cells in Cairo, Matariya, Ismailia, Beni Suef, Daqhalia (specifically Mansoura), Kafr al-Sheikh, Sharqia, 6th of October, Fayoum, Qena, and Giza. A number of parallel, functionally oriented, cellular structures tied these groups together. These included groups specializing in media production, engineering (i.e., mechanical aspects of improvised explosive device (IED) construction, rocket propulsion, and aerodynamics), chemical engineering (i.e., production of efficient explosive compounds), and weapons storage. Ancillary cells, like those specializing in reconnaissance, training, and road observation, were also likely formed on an ad hoc basis. Absorbed into the organization were elements of other, independently operating groups like Tawhid wal-Jihad and al-Furqan Brigades, both of which had their own complex cellular structures and operational knowledge. (TIMEP has separately profiled Tawhid wal-Jihad and Kitaa'ib al-Furqan.)

The organization's current structure, and whether any internal changes have occurred, is unclear. Two possible transformative influences include ABM's organizational affiliations (with Gaza factions, al-Qaeda, and, most recently, the Islamic State) and the activities of security services, the potency of which has evolved markedly over the past four years. Despite this, the group's ongoing attacks in the greater Cairo area may suggest that some of these elements— i.e., those outside of its North Sinai stronghold—remain active.

Wilayat Sinai's particular structural design portended sustained counterterrorism activity. According to sources, the organization's recruitment cycle included a rigorous vetting process—one which was originally overseen by deputy head Muhammad Nasif. Nasif also tasked his recruits with changing their names, severing their relationships with people outside the group, disposing of their cell phones and other trackable means of communication, and avoiding prayer in mosques. To prevent structural collapse in the event of a breach, members were compartmentalized—and their knowledge of other members' identities was confined to the cell of which they were a part.

ABM also had in its ranks a relatively large amount of intellectual capital, with many of its members having valuable educational, vocational, and military or paramilitary experience. This especially benefited ABM's functional cells, like those tasked with reconnaissance and IED construction. For example, after engineering graduate Hossam Ali Farghali was vetted and recruited, he took an ABM "workshop" on projectile composition and manufacturing, and was tasked by Muhammad Nasif with utilizing aerodynamic formulae to increase the range of its rockets, so as to more easily hit Israel. Additionally, some of its leaders, like al-Furqan head Muhammad Ahmed Nasr Muhammad, mastermind of the 2013 Suez Canal attack, held advanced degrees (ironically, his was a Ph.D. in Suez Canal development). Not all of the leadership had these credentials, however. Tawfik Freij Ziyada, for example, was a honey salesman by trade.

Prior military and police experience bolstered their operational aptitude. Special forces officer Hisham Ali Ashmawy, a former ABM training official and the current head of the al-Qaeda-affiliated group al-Morabitoon, brought to the organization specialized knowledge of irregular warfare and military counterterrorism tactics. Hisham used his expertise in explosives to mastermind some of ABM's most high-profile attacks, including the attempted assassination of Interior Minister Mohamed Ibrahim in 2013. (Incidentally, the suicide bomber who actually carried out the attack was another military officer, Major Waleed Badr.)

Major Emad al-Din Ahmed Abdel Hameed, Hisham's deputy head of training and fellow operational planner at ABM, was also involved in the assassination attempt. Similarly, policemen-turned-informants Lieutenant Muhammad Muhammad Eweis Muhammadand Colonel Sameh Ahmed al-Azizi handed over sensitive information that ostensibly helped with other attacks; for example, authorities discovered on the lieutenant's personal computer a list of police officers and home addresses. Former naval officer Ahmed Amr, likewise, played a key role in Wilayat Sinai's November 2014 attack on Egyptian naval vessels off the coast of Damietta.

The organization has a range of weapons capabilities. It has an assortment of light arms, man-portable air defense systems (MANPADS), rocket-propelled grenades, and 60-mm mortars. More recently, the group showcased its possession of, and ability to effectively use, Katyusha rockets and Kornet anti-tank missiles, both Russian-manufactured weapons. The origin of its armaments is not altogether clear, although Gaza and Libya are likely sources—as are weapons taken from Bedouin stockpiles and Egyptian security forces.

Their weapons may also be entering Egypt from its southern border with Sudan. Interestingly, Kitaa'ib al-Furqan reportedly smuggled across the Egyptian-Sudanese border 10 Katyusha rockets some time ago; they hid the rockets at a location in Giza, and then likely moved them to a storage site in Sharqia.

Despite this variety, Wilayat Sinai most commonly uses basic IEDs. The organization first used crude explosives when it launched its debut attack on gas distribution infrastructure in 2011. But since then, its construction of these devices—and its refinement of their composition materials—have probably grown in complexity. The organization has demonstrated its ability to effectively use IEDs to attack soft targets, including mobile military and police patrols. It has also employed larger explosives, often in the form of vehicle-borne improvised explosive devices (VBIEDs, or car bombs), to attack hardened structures, such as security directorates, police stations, and, most recently, a diplomatic mission. Cellular and timed detonation devices (which can be delayed up to a month), and, likely, pressure-sensitive detonators, are among their capabilities.

Funding for ABM weapons and operations is, of yet, largely unknown, although smuggling and other criminal activity are a likely source. One of its early sources of funding was Muhammad Ahmed al-Adawi Shalbaya, the owner of a Daqhalia export-import business who reportedly sent the group LE1.7 million through bank transfers from Saudi Arabia. Whether there presently exists a money pipeline between Wilayat Sinai and the Islamic State, or between it and other entities, is unclear, however.

Abu Osama al-Masry, a senior-level ABM leader, showed an early interest in the Islamic State, going back to July 2014, when he praised the Islamic State's actions and ideology in an Eid al-Fitr sermon, foreshadowing the eventual alliance of the two groups. Al-Masry trained with factions in Gaza Strip, accessing it through border tunnels, and fought for some time in Syria. Based on voice comparison, he appears to be the blurred figure in a video released in November 2015.

Shadi Meneai's involvement with Ansar Bayt al-Maqdis has been disputed. Egyptian security forces claimed to have killed Meneai, whom they described as the "leader" of Ansar Bayt al-Maqdis, in a May 2014 raid. ABM, however, vehemently denied both Meneai's death and his having been the leader of the group, and he later appeared in a video reading his own eulogy. Meneai does appear to be among the group's senior leadership, however; he is a former smuggler whose father is a Sawarka tribesman and who was part of the ABM's early attacks on gas infrastructure. Turabeen Sheikh Musa al-Dalh offered a million-pound reward for Meneai on May 2, 2015, following an attack on Turabeen tribesman Ibrahim Ergani's Sinai home.

Kamal Alam, described as a senior leader in the group's organization, was reportedly killed during a January 2014 counterterrorism operation. (While reports indicated that Alam was featured in photos from "Mujahid Diary", photo comparison showed this to be incorrect.) He reportedly fought in both Syria and Libya.

Ahmed Salam Mabruk is a longtime militant with a history in violent extremism across the region, and he has strong ties to Ayman al-Zawahiri and al-Qaeda. Mabruk was extradited to Egypt as part of the infamous Returnees from Albania case in 1999, where he faced charges related to his activity with al-Gamaa al-Islamiya, one of Egypt's most active extremist groups in the 1990s. Since his 2012 release from prison, Egyptian officials have suggested that Mabruk played a leadership role in ABM.

Since its formation, judged to be at some point in 2011, the group appears to have breathed life into Egyptian jihadi cells by bringing them under one umbrella. This has been evidenced by the leadership of the group, many of whom are experienced militants who had previously been a part of other groups, particularly Tawhid wal-Jihad and the Mujahideen Shura Council (MSC) in the Environs of Jerusalem. When Israel killed Tawhid wal-Jihad/MSC leaders in 2012, Ansar Bayt al-Maqdis vowed retribution.

Early on, the group ingratiated itself to the local population, calling on them to stand with ABM in its fight against the state. ABM's early attacks on Sinai gas infrastructure were used as a means of rallying this support. In fliers passed out to locals, they reportedly stated: "If you are not with us, do not be against us." And, in another statement, they described themselves as "your brothers...men from [Egypt]...perhaps your neighbors or relatives."

On April 9, 2014, the U.S. Department of State declared Ansar Bayt al-Maqdis a terrorist organization. Egypt followed suit shortly thereafter. On November 10, 2014, Ansar Bayt al-Maqdis formally swore allegiance (bay'a) to the Islamic State, changing its name to Wilayat Sinai (Province of Sinai). This allegiance provides the Islamic State with a nominal presence in Sinai, while, in theory, also providing Ansar Bayt al-Maqdis with greater resources. How and to what extent this has materialized is unclear, however.

Egyptian security forces have carried out a number of operations against Wilayat Sinai. The most recent and largest of these was the September 2015 Operation Martyr's Right, during which the military claimed to have killed over 500 operatives and arrested at least 600. While Israel's role in combating the organization is unclear, WS has claimed that Israeli drones flying over Sinai have killed its operatives. Notwithstanding these claims, Egyptian authorities vehemently deny penetration of their airspace. In any case, despite these setbacks, the organization's activity has only grown in ability, complexity, and magnitude.

Following an attack on the Italian Consulate on July 11, 2015, it appears that a mainland branch of the Islamic State emerged. An attack claim was published in the same standard format as Islamic State claims throughout the region; but, instead of attributing the attack to Islamic State Wilayat Sinai, the claim attributed the attack to Islamic State "Misr" (Egypt). Four other claims have since been made in the same manner. While it is possible that one of ABM's previous regional cells could have resumed operations in Cairo under that name, there is currently no evidence to substantiate this.

Jewish population in nearby Israel, where the majority of the group's efforts were focused (with the exception of pipeline attacks in Egypt). Soon after the removal of President Muhammad Morsi, however, Ansar Bayt al-Maqdis shifted its attention to the Egyptian government for waging war against Islam. Since aligning themselves with the Islamic State and becoming Wilayat Sinai, the group has adopted some, but not all of the Islamic State's ideology. The act of beheading enemies, especially those they deem as traitors, has become more frequent since the group pledged bay'a to the Islamic State, showing a clear evolution of their practices.

Both Wilayat Sinai and its predecessor have claimed attacks on international targets. These include, for example, an attack on a bus full of Korean tourists near Taba, the bombing of Italy's consulate in Cairo, and the killing of American oil worker William Henderson. The propaganda that surrounded the beheading of Croatian Tomislav Salopek and that that followed the downed Russian aircraft appear to show the growing transnationalization of the organization's operations. At the very least, these attacks show a superficial strategic alignment with the Islamic State, but they may also represent a focus on attacking the Egyptian economy.

The group claimed responsibility for several attacks on natural gas pipelines, as far back as February 5, 2011, and as late as January 17, 2014. In a coordinated attack on August 18, 2011, the group targeted a bus in Eilat, Israel, killing at least eight Israelis and three members of the Egyptian security forces.

On September 5, 2013, Ansar Bayt al-Maqdis unsuccessfully attempted to assassinate Mohamed Ibrahim, Egypt's Interior Minister. On December 24, 2013, the group attacked the Mansoura Security Directorate. This remains one of the deadliest attacks in Egypt in the past decade; sixteen people were killed and 134 were injured in the bombing. This bombing also represented a moment of intense escalation in the Egyptian government's "war on terror;" despite not having been connected with the attack, the Muslim Brotherhood were declared a terrorist group the following day.

Following the Mansoura attack, ABM released footage of them apparently shooting down a helicopter. Militants used a man-portable air-defense system to take down the aircraft, killing the five men on board. In its first attack on tourists, a suicide bomber attacked a bus of South Korean tourists traveling near the Israeli border on February 16, 2014. The attack killed three of the tourists and the Egyptian bus driver.

The group launched a campaign against Israel during a period of intense conflict between Israel and Gaza in July 2014. The group released videos of Grad and 107-mm rocket attacks on the Israeli town of Eilat, two attacks on the village Bnei Netzarim, and one on another cross-border location.

In August 2014, Ansar Bayt al-Maqdis turned its attention back to Egypt. The group released a video first documenting the murder of Egyptian police on August 18. Ten days later, on August 28, the group released a video in which they document the beheading of four Egyptian men they accuse of collaboration with Israeli intelligence. The August beheadings were the first violence of this type for the group, marking a chilling change in tactic that has endured through the posting of this profile in November 2015.

On October 24, 2014, Ansar Bayt al-Maqdis carried out what was its deadliest attack up until that point. The group detonated a car bomb at a heavily guarded security checkpoint in Sheikh Zuweid and then ambushed the guards who came to investigate the attack. Later the same day, they opened fire on a security checkpoint in Arish. The attacks killed at least 33 Egyptian security personnel and wounded at least as many. This was the at that point the deadliest attack on the Egyptian military in decades.

In December 2014, Wilayat Sinai claimed responsibility for the death of American oil worker William Henderson. The group produced pictures taken of his identification cards following his death. This act of targeting a Westerner, combined with the recent adoption of beheading as a tactic, has caused some worry that this was evidence on an ideological shift that would mirror the more extreme Islamic State ideology.

On January 29, 2015, Wilayat Sinai carried out an attack reminiscent of its earlier October 2014 strike against the military. The group utilized suicide bombers, car bombs, mortars, and intense gunfire against a military base and nearby security buildings, a hotel, a police club, a newspaper office, and various security checkpoints through North Sinai. The result was over 30 dead Egyptian military members and many more wounded. The scale and immense coordination of the attacks, along with the general escalation of their ability to strike at military targets, pointed toward the group's overall cohesion.

A suicide bomber attempted to drive a stolen water tanker into police barracks in Arish (a city in North Sinai and site of ongoing conflict between militants and the Egyptian military) on March 10, 2015. The tanker exploded before entering the barracks after police opened fire. At least 42 officers were wounded and a civilian was killed.

On April 2, 2015, militants opened fire in simultaneous attacks on two checkpoints in Sheikh Zuweid and near Arish. Five Egyptian soldiers and two civilians were killed while 19 security personnel and 10 civilians were injured. WS claimed responsibility for three separate attacks targeting security personnel on April 12, 2015. An armored vehicle was attacked on the highway killing six security personnel and injuring two. Later, a car bomb exploded near the police station in Arish killing six people and injuring 40 others. Militants later opened fire at a checkpoint in Rafah, injuring three security personnel.

WS appeared to have briefly gained control over parts of Sheikh Zuweid on July 1, 2015, after coordinating attacks on 21 security facilities and checkpoints. According to a statement by the Supreme Council of the Armed Forces, 17 members of the armed forces were killed, while militants reported these numbers to be over 100.

WS released a statement claiming responsibility for a rocket attack on an Egyptian naval vessel in the Mediterranean on July 16, 2015. The Egyptian army claimed that the patrol boat had exchanged fire with militants off the coast of Rafah causing the boat to catch fire.

WS took captive Tamislov Salopek, a Croatian citizen and employee of CGG Ardiseis, on July 24, 2015. The group released a video on August 5, 2015, threatening to kill Salopek if Egypt did not release all female Muslim prisoners within 48 hours. A video circulated on August 12, 2015 with a photo of Salopek decapitated.

On September 16 and 19, 2015, militants opened fire and killed Major General Khaled Kamal Osman and Brigadier General Ahmed Abdel Satar. WS operatives shot and killed prominent Sawarka tribesman Khaled El-Menaei on October 1, 2015.

On October 31, 2015, a Russian commercial aircraft carrying 224 mostly Russian citizens crashed in the Sinai. WS claimed the attack on its social media accounts, but did not elaborate on the manner by which it brought the plane down. Immediately following its claim, the group carried out a car bombing against the Arish police club and beheaded Gomaa Shahada, a local accused of collaborating with security forces, showing the group's ability to use its media attention to its advantage.

Jaysh al-Islam

The group primarily attacks civilian targets via kidnappings and bombings. The group has also been known to launch rockets into Israel.Mumtaz Dughmush – Dughmush, also known as Abou Abir, is a leader of the Dughmush clan of Gaza City and a former member of the Hamas party.

Jaysh al-Islam was founded by Dughmush in 2006. On May 19, 2011, the United States designated Jaysh al-Islam a terrorist organization. journalist Alan Johnston, Jaysh al-Islam condemned the occupation of Palestine and held the British responsible for the creation of the state of Israel; the group also condemned the United States as taking part in a crusade against Islam. In this statement, Jaysh al-Islam explicitly stated that there is no difference between the governments of these countries and their people "whose bloody and money are free for the taking."

The group desires the destruction of nations and the establishment of an Islamic caliphate, and it has publicly praised Al Qaeda and Osama Bin Laden. The group also has worked to carry out attacks with the Mujahideen Shura Council in the Environs of Jerusalem (MSC).

While Jaysh al-Islam has carried out operations with Hamas' militant wing, the Al Qassem Brigades, Dughmush has particularly challenged Hamas' authority, and the two groups have been in serious conflict since as early as 2007. Johnston was kidnapped as a hostage to be used in negotiations aiming for the release of Jaysh al-Islam operatives arrested by Hamas and for the release of Abu Qatada al-Filistini, an Islamic cleric held in Britain. The kidnapping led to months of Hamas attacks on Jaysh al-Islam strongholds.

Three months into Johnston's arrest, Jaysh al-Islam issued a message to the Al Qassem brigades, praising them for their actions in the Gaza strip, declaring that they would stand behind the group if they were to announce the establishment of an Islamic caliphate, and asking them not to request for Johnston's release.

On June 25 2006, Jaysh al-Islam cooperated with the Al Qassem Brigades and the Popular Resistance Committees (PRC) in the infamous kidnapping of Israel Defense Forces soldier Gilad Shalit. Jaysh al-Islam announced in July 2007, however, that after kidnapping him, the group had handed Shalit over to Hamas.

In August of that year, the group kidnapped two Fox News correspondents and held them in Gaza; this was the longest duration hostages had been held in the territory until that time. While the kidnapping was originally claimed by the unknown "Holy Jihad Brigade," it was later attributed to Jaysh al-Islam.

On March 20, 2007, Jaysh al-Islam made headlines when they kidnapped BBC journalist Alan Johnston in Gaza. In a video released by the group, they featured journalist Alan Johnston in captivity, with a suicide belt strapped to his waist and asking for intervention to prevent his imminent death. He was eventually freed on July 4, 2007, days after Hamas seized full control of Gaza.

The Egyptian Ministry of Interior blamed a New Years Eve 2011 attack on a Christian church on Jaysh al-Islam. The group denied the attack, which killed 21 church-goers in Alexandria.

An August 5, 2012 attack on a group of Egyptian army soldiers preparing to break their Ramadan fast was credited to Jaysh al-Islam. Although others attributed this attack to the MSC, the group denied responsibility.

Al-Furqan Brigades

Throughout Egypt, with operational centers in Cairo and Ismailia. The group typically carries out targeted attacks and publicizes these through social media. According to investigations from Egypian National Security, the group has received significant funding and training from the al-Qassem Brigades in Gaza.

The group's founders are alleged to be Hany Mustafa Amen Amer Mahmoud and Mohamed Ahmed Nasr Mohamed, also known as Abou Ahmed al-Haj. While very little is known publicly about the group, Egyptian National Security has launched extensive investigations into the group since their infamous 2013 attack on ships in the Suez Canal.

It clear from the prosecutor's investigations that the group is operating in conjunction with Ansar Bayt al-Maqdis, however the level of integration between the two groups is unclear, and Kitab al-Furqan releases their own media.

The group views the current government as illegitimate as it does not apply shari'a law, and therefore they believe they are justified in armed resistance, conducting attacks against any state actors or institutions (including media).The group has also claimed that it views the path to righteousness as through the "ammunition box, not the ballot box."

In September 2013, the group released a video showing two of its operatives firing rocket-propelled grenades at merchant ships in the Suez Canal in July and August of that year.On October 7, 2013, the group launched two rocket-propelled grenades at a satellite station in the Cairo suburb of Maadi. The group has also released numerous videos detailing targeted shootings against state security.

Jund al-Islam

According to reports from Police General Hani Zaher and terror expert Maher Ferghali, Jund al-Islam is in possession of advanced weaponry, including rocket-propelled grenades (RPGs) and anti-aircraft missiles. In their one known attack, the group employed RPGs and two vehicles loaded with explosives.

Jund al-Islam was widely unknown before 2011, however both Zaher and Ferghali have indicated that Jund al-Islam conducted a military show on the day of Osama Bin Laden's death in May of that year. Four months later, on September 11, they claimed a large attack on a military intelligence building in Rafah.

In a statement claiming responsibility for the September 11 attack, Jund al-Islam denounced the Egyptian military as traitors to Islam and held them responsible for crimes committed in the interest of "the Jews." Although this statement was the only official Jund al-Islam proclamation, the timing of the military show and the military intelligence attack suggests at least a loyalty to Al-Qaeda.

The September 11, 2013 attack on the Rafah intelligence building killed at least six people and injured 17 more, including 7 civilians.

Takfeer wal-Hegra

The group wears black masks and carries black flags bearing the confession: "There is no god but God." The group is known to be well-organized and in possession of highly-advanced weapons. Abdel-Fattah Hasan Hussein Salem—Salem was arrested with an aide in October 2013.Mohamed Eid al-Tihi—Tihi was arrested on November 13, 2011; sources claimed he died in a Cairo prison in February 2012.

An earlier iteration of the group was led by Shokri Mustafa, who became radicalized in Egypt's prisons during his imprisonment from 1965 to 1971; Mustafa was executed in 1977 after the group assassinated Muhammad al-Dhahbi, the former Minister of Waqf. At this time the group was largely driven underground.

However, the downfall of Mubarak in 2011 marked the emergence of a new entity calling themselves Takfir wal-Hijra, in the Sinai. Other than their reprise of Takfir wal-Hijra ideology and tactics, this group does not appear to have any substantial connections with the Takfir wal-Hijra of the 1970s.

While there has been some limited evidence to suggest the presence of Takfir wal-Hijra "networks" in the Middle East and North Africa throughout the period after 1977, there is no evidence to indicate anything but a nominal relationship between these groups and either the earlier or later group operating in Egypt.

The group adheres to a particularly extreme interpretation of Sayid Qutb's teachings. This interpretation claims as apostates nearly all who are not themselves members of the group, including all state leaders who do not govern under a strict interpretation of shari'a, any peoples governed by such leaders and thus complicit in their leadership, and any religious leader who does not condemn such leaders as apostates.

In November 2011, a raid on a Takfir wal-Hijra hideout resulted in the death of one police officer. While Takfir wal-Hijra has not explicitly claimed attacks in recent years, groups with similar tactics and characteristics have enacted attacks in Sinai, including attacks on January 29 and February 7, 2011. Reports indicated that dozens of men carrying machine guns, rocket-propelled grenades, and other arms attacked a police station in Sheikh Zuweid, leaving five dead in the January incident, and injured two at a police barracks in Rafah in the later one.